W9-BGG-750

A Lighthearted Look at Life From

POST SCRIPTS

From The Saturday Evening Post

Edited by Tina Hacker

Hallmark Editions

Hallmark Cards, Inc., Kansas City, Missouri.
Printed in the United States of America.
Library of Congress Catalog Card Number: 74-28621.
Standard Book Number: 87529-438-3.

POST SCRIPTS

1.

2.

3.

Let Me Write That Down

"Let's see, now. I want two hamburgers with sauce, but no onions; two with onions, but no sauce; two with pickle and just a little sauce; and one with nothing at all — just plain. I also want five coffees: two with just cream, two with sugar and no cream, and one black. Then, I want one limeade with no ice, two hot chocolates — one with a lot of whipped cream and one with not very much — one double and one regular vanilla — "

Vernon H. Kurtz

Stop the World and I'll Get Right Off

"So you're finally going to paint the house? Say, that's swell! Frankly, I've wondered how long you'd be able to stand that crumby color. Now you can really — Oh. You mean you're painting the inside. Not the outside? ... Oh .... Oh, I see. Well — "

"Boy, get a whiff of that beef cooking! We certainly came to the right house for dinner! Ribs? Now, look, you shouldn't have gone to all that expense; though I'll admit, just the thought of a big pink, juicy slab of prime rib really makes my mouth wat — Oh. Short ribs.... Oh, I see. Well — "

Pat McQuesten

From the Cynic's Dictionary

Synonym. A word you can't think of when you can't think of the word you want.

Lester V. Berrey

Teen-Age Standard Time

1:45 A.M.: "Late? It's only a little past midnight. Jeepers, if I have to break up the party, check out my date and be home for bed at practically sundown — well, I might as well start dating girls Amy's age." (Amy is his sister, age 3½ .)

11:05 A.M.: "Hey, it's almost noon. How's for lunch? I haven't tasted food since breakfast and I'm starving, man, starving!" (He ate breakfast at 10:30.)

7:42 P.M.: (MALE) "Stop fretting, parent. Play it casual. I got plenty time to shower and dress. I'm not supposed to pick Nancy up for hours yet." (He's supposed to pick Nancy up at eight.)

(FEMALE) "Everybody come help me — PLEASE! I can't find but one of my red ballet slippers and I'll die — but Die if I have to wear the white ones, and Pete is supposed to pick me up any minute now — ANY MINUTE!" (Pete is supposed to pick her up at 8:30.)

4:45 P.M.: "Tying up the phone? Joanie and *me?* Why, Joanie didn't even *call* me until just a little while ago." (Joanie called her at 2:05.)

10:20 A.M.: "Get up? Now? At DAWN?"

So He Says

This is a short cut: The backhanded apology for being seventeen miles off course on an eighteen-mile trip.

First thing tomorrow: A purely imaginary time at which all necessary repairs in the house and all chores on the place are to be done.

Hi: Tender greeting after six months' separation.

Bringing home a few friends for dinner: Chaos, caused by stampede of ravenous beasts.

Nancy D. Sinkler

Ideas I Never Should've Had

"You act as though removing one little screw is going to cause the entire camera to fall to pieces. In order to put your fears to rest, I'm removing this one insignificant little screw from this circular thing, and I'm — "

"Just to prove to you that drying the dishes isn't any bowl of cherries, I'll wash for a change, and you dry."

"O.K., kid, burn one in to me! Put 'er right there in the old mitt, kid — right in the old — "

Vernon H. Kurtz

Old Furniture

About the time it's half refinished,
My enthusiasm has diminished.

A. A. Lattimer

Some Rather Unfortunate Headlines

GAME AND FISH HEAD RETIRES

GOVERNOR NOT IMPRESSED BY DAM SITE

STATE U. TEAM HONORED IN BRIEF CEREMONEY

Charles Matteson

"Stop me if you've heard this one!"

Home Bulletins

Cut Out, Pin Up

For the Kitchen

This dessert is for tonight.
Don't take even a LITTLE bite.
(Those whose hunger is utterly utter
May fill themselves up on peanut butter.)

For Mamma's Desk

Letters must be answered at least once
Every six munce.

For the Kiddies' Room

Darling children, we implore you:
Use the shelves that we built for you
Not to climb, and not to bunk on —
But to put away your junk on.

For Over the Studio Couch

If to jump on this you choose
Kindly, first, remove your shoes.

Virginia Brasier

Gardener's Song

I spaded and shoveled and planted the seeds.
Now things in my garden are growing like weeds.
There's only one trouble I've noticed so far:
Weeds are what ninety percent of them are!

Georgie Starbuck Galbraith

"Let us face facts — it's *empty!*"

"Just ads."

"Absolutely nothing could happen today to make it worth this."

Definitions That May Be Right or May Not

Dogmatic:	A sort of revolver carried by police dogs.
Pseudonym:	A nym that is not your real nym.
Summary:	Nice and warm.
Gallfly:	A fly with some nerve.

John Bailey

Don't Worry

Camp Luckee-Lassie
August 13 I think

Dear Mother and Daddy.

This isnt the time they make you write home to your parents but I am anyway. Gail Padderson is in my cabin and I hate her quite a bit but I have a new friend name Marlene. Shes teen and wears lipstick. When the consulers dont see her.

The horses all knew me and Injun threw me just like he did last year but I wasn hurt much. You shoudnt have worried so much about my clothes because I got plenty. becouse I only been wearing the white T shirt and my jeans. See I am saving you the washing ha ha. My money is lasting o.k. but I may make some mocksuns, then I will need $3.65. I never found my toothbrush but it is only 3 more days and I am not going to waste my good money. Since I got one at home.

Give the hamsters a kiss for me and also each other. Marlene is homesick and cries but Im not. Except at night. But I havent cried yet just allmost. We went on a hike yesterday but it rained and oh mother the food is just Pew. The kids in Owlet cabin say Ugg but our cabin says Pew.

Dont worry about me.

Lots of love,

Your daughter,

Paula Jean M.

Kay Nelson

d, the drainage is wonderful."

Argument

s of tongue or pen
ou've counted ten!

Dick Kardel

How White Was My Elephant!

The day of the wedding approaches,
The presents pour in for the bride:
A ring of the bell and a feminine yell,
And another is being untied.

Suffused by the joy of the soon-to-be Mrs.,
You eagerly murmur, "I wonder what this is!"
And when you've unwrapped it and ogled your fill,
You find yourself gloomily wondering still.

You twist it and turn it in twenty directions,
You paw through the box for additional sections,
You grope for instructions, you search for a label,
You pile the excelsior high on the table,
And wonder what manner of mortal could bring
This so inexcusable,
Painfully sizable,
Plainly unusable,
Unanalyzable
Thing!

Thank you so much for the Whoozit,
Dear Mrs. Horace McFee;
You're really too kind to have bothered to find
A present for poor little me.
I'll think of you constantly, darling,
Whenever I happen to use it.
You've always been graced with such different taste!
Thank you again for the Whoozit.

W. W. Watt

Summer Summary

When vacation is over, you'll often find,
As you give it a backward look,
You could have made out with half the clothes
And twice the money you took.

Stephen Schlitzer

They're Fixed, of Course

Contests are gyps, and wicked as sin —
I never win.

Helen Castle

The Mornings Come Early This Year

It's now 8:10 and I should rise,
But I believe I'll shut my eyes
Till 8:15, because I'll save
Five minutes if I miss my shave.
I'm sure there isn't any news.
I'll skip the radio and snooze
Till 8:18 and then get dressed.
I'll wear my tweed — it still looks pressed —
And last night's shirt seemed clean to me.
Not changing clothes will save me three
Full minutes, so that I can snore
Serenely till 8:24.
In fact, cold coffee suits me fine,
I'll sleep until 8:29,
And then perhaps a softer egg —
O.K., O.K., leggo my leg!

Loyd Rosenfield

Vacatio

My dear Aun
How nice to
You're righ
Where tou
Because t
Just perf
We get t
I think
In fact,
Just le
We'd
But,
You
Rel
To
Y

"On the other ha

No

The saddest wor
Are those before

Open Letter to Doctor Widge

Dear Doctor Widge: For two years now I have been in receipt of a bill from you which simply says: "Dr. Widge. Professional Services: $5.00. Westfield, Mass."

For brevity and consistency, I hand you, sir, the palm. Never in those two years have you added a thing to your simple statement. It is too bad too. Because I have never known a Doctor Widge and I have never been in Westfield. Furthermore, I have not had professional services since four years ago, when my wife kicked me under a bridge table.

I mean I cannot see why I am entitled to your monthly attention. Not that I mind it. In dull moments on rainy days I sit back with my eyes shut, puff on my pipe and wonder what Doctor Widge looks like. Is he a tall, fat man with glasses? Is he a short, round man? Or is he oblong? Or possibly triangular? What is his office like? Modern? Ancient? Has he any new magazines in the waiting room?

Doctor Widge, I know this will come as a shock, but I hate to hold you in suspense, probably betting with your nurse as to whether I will ever pay the bill or not.

Frankly, I won't pay it. Why? Because I never incurred it and I don't owe it. Even if I did, I'm afraid you'd have trouble.

You see, you're not the only guy who's been sending me bills for months. But you are unique and wonderful. You are the only one I don't owe!

Your phantom patient,

Robert Fontaine

Footnotes on a National League Scorecard

(By W. Shakespeare)

It appears no other thing to me than a foul....

Hamlet: Act ii, sc. 2

Out, I say!

Macbeth: Act v, sc. 1

O hateful error...!

Julius Caesar: Act v, sc. 3

The game is up.

Cymbeline: Act iii, sc. 3

Play out the play.

King Henry IV, Part I: Act ii, sc. 4

Caesar's wing
Will make him fly an ordinary pitch.

Julius Caesar: Act i, sc. 1

A hit, a very palpable hit.

Hamlet: Act v, sc. 2

Double, double...

Macbeth: Act iv, sc. 1

Let him show himself what he is and steal...

Much Ado About Nothing: Act iii, sc. 3

Put it home.

Othello: Act v, sc. 1

How White Was My Elephant!

The day of the wedding approaches,
The presents pour in for the bride:
A ring of the bell and a feminine yell,
And another is being untied.

Suffused by the joy of the soon-to-be Mrs.,
You eagerly murmur, "I wonder what this is!"
And when you've unwrapped it and ogled your fill,
You find yourself gloomily wondering still.

You twist it and turn it in twenty directions,
You paw through the box for additional sections,
You grope for instructions, you search for a label,
You pile the excelsior high on the table,
And wonder what manner of mortal could bring
This so inexcusable,
Painfully sizable,
Plainly unusable,
Unanalyzable
Thing!

Thank you so much for the Whoozit,
Dear Mrs. Horace McFee;
You're really too kind to have bothered to find
A present for poor little me.
I'll think of you constantly, darling,
Whenever I happen to use it.
You've always been graced with such different taste!
Thank you again for the Whoozit.

W. W. Watt

Summer Summary

When vacation is over, you'll often find,
As you give it a backward look,
You could have made out with half the clothes
And twice the money you took.

Stephen Schlitzer

They're Fixed, of Course

Contests are gyps, and wicked as sin –
I never win.

Helen Castle

The Mornings Come Early This Year

It's now 8:10 and I should rise,
But I believe I'll shut my eyes
Till 8:15, because I'll save
Five minutes if I miss my shave.
I'm sure there isn't any news.
I'll skip the radio and snooze
Till 8:18 and then get dressed.
I'll wear my tweed – it still looks pressed –
And last night's shirt seemed clean to me.
Not changing clothes will save me three
Full minutes, so that I can snore
Serenely till 8:24.
In fact, cold coffee suits me fine,
I'll sleep until 8:29,
And then perhaps a softer egg –
O.K., O.K., leggo my leg!

Loyd Rosenfield

Vacation From Vacationers

My dear Aunt Jane and Uncle Jack:
How nice to hear you're coming back;
You're right, it's heaven to reside
Where tourists all return like tide
Because the air is mild and pure –
Just perfect for our guided tour;
We get to see each friend we knew –
I think we've seen all *their* friends too;
In fact, your cousins' chums, the Meeks,
Just left here after several weeks;
We'd love to welcome you again
But, most unfortunately, when
You get down here we'll be up there
Relaxing in your smoggy air;
Too bad – we've always so enjoyed
Your yearly visits. Love from Loyd.

Loyd Rosenfield

"George always did have a gift for turning a phrase."

"On the other hand, the drainage is wonderful."

No Argument

The saddest words of tongue or pen
Are those before you've counted ten!

Dick Kardel

"I gave him away!"

Punch Lines From Some Anecdotes Which I Wish I'd Never Listened To

"...To really appreciate the story, though, I guess you have to know old Tom for the character he is. He has a dry sort of humor you have to live with a while before you can understand it."

"...but, actually, the funniest thing about it was the expression on his face when he said it."

"...but the real joke of it was that all of us who work with him have heard him complain a hundred times about that very same sort of thing."

Ralph Reppert

The Conventiongoer's Guide, Sort Of

OFFICIAL PROGRAM *Saturday*	ACTUAL PROGRAM *Saturday*
9:00 A.M.: Registration, Parlor G, Mezzanine Floor, Hotel Middleville.	9:00 A.M.: Flat Tire, Wrong Road, 46 Miles Out of Middleville.
11:00 A.M.: Meeting Members and Auxiliary, East Room; Call to Order by President; Official Greetings.	11:00 A.M.: Meeting in Lobby With Arnold Heeple, Old Buddy; Call to Mike's Place, Very Dry.
1:15 P.M.: Meeting Resolutions and Credentials Committees; Report of Statistical Chairman.	1:15 P.M.: Lunch. Get Spare Fixed.
2:40 P.M.: Address by H. Saplind Onway: Importance of Co-ordinated Effort in Community Living.	2:40 P.M.: Registration. Call up Friends of Friends. Nap.
7:45 P.M.: Cocktail Party in Whee Room; Dinner Dance.	7:45 P.M.: Cocktail Party in Whee Room; Dinner Dance.

Sunday
7:15 A.M. Sharp: Conducted Tour of Points of Local Interest. Including Inspection New Locomotive Roundhouse.

11:15 A.M.: Sere Room, Address by Regional Chairman: Wake up, Members, for the Time is Now!

2:00 P.M.: Drum and Bugle Contest, Public Schools Stadium.

4:00 P.M.: Adjournment.

Monday
9:00 A.M.: West Room, Report of Year's Progress; Special Committees.

11:30 A.M.: Parlor G, Outgoing President's Address: What of the Future, Fellows?

3:30 P.M.: Special Committees. Election of Officers. Adjournment.

Sunday
7:15 A.M. Sharp: Turn Over.

11:15 A.M.: Turn Back Over.

2:00 P.M.: Conducted Tour of Points of Local Interest; Arnold Heeple, Group Chairman; Write Check.

4:00 P.M.: Start.

Monday
9:00 A.M.: Cold Shower. More Coffee.

11:30 A.M.: Financial Report in Own Room: Where Did That Other $24 Go?

3:30 P.M.: Cold Shower. Adjournment!

John I. Keasler

Answers to Some Common Questions

If you have a boy approaching the 8-12 age class, this is going to prove a lot more useful than you realize. Simply clip it out and present it to him on his 8th birthday:

1. I have never seen a live dinosaur.
2. Even the strongest man in the world cannot lift the battleship USS Missouri.
3. The Indian wars were pretty well over when I was a boy.
4. Our car will not go 165 miles an hour.
5. There is no possibility that in some years we may have two Christmases.

Otto Janssen

Exam Day

"Backward, turn backward,
O Time, in your flight."
And tell me just one thing
I studied last night!

Marguerite Frazier

Food for Thought

To market, to market
To buy a thick roast;
Home again, home again,
Wieners to toast!

Colleen Hynes Johnson

"Mind if I use the car myself tonight? I'm taking your mother out and I want to impress her."

Movie Version

Picture, picture, on the screen,
How I long to flee you.
Tell me, truly, do you know
Why I came to see you?

Philip Lazarus

Helpful Hints, or Anyway Hints, for Parents

In attempting to control children with oral commands and admonitions and yelling, the phraseology used is all-important. Here are a number of time-tested phrases which were addressed to me as a child, now made available in this limited edition to parents of the new generation.

1. I WANT PERFECT PEACE AND QUIET AROUND THIS PLACE.

2. YOU'RE OLDER THAN THE OTHER CHILDREN AND SHOULD SET THEM AN EXAMPLE.

3. I WANT THIS CONSTANT BICKERING TO STOP.

4. THE LEAST I CAN EXPECT IS SOME CONSIDERATION.

5. I'VE FINALLY GOT THE HOUSE IN ORDER AND I WANT IT KEPT THAT WAY.

John Swartwout

Telltale Signs

Chalked on a sidewalk (1948):

Jimmy Carter Hates Girls.

Written on a fence (1950):

JIM CARTER THINKS NANCY LEE JONES IS A JERK!

Inscribed on a book cover (1952):

Carter says: Down with wommen!

Painted on a Model A (1954):

NO FEMALES ALLOWED

Carved on a tree trunk (1957):

Engraved inside a platinum ring (1959):

J.C. to N.L.J.— All my love — June 6, 1959

Kay Nelson

Don't Love That Neighbor

The party pest we'd list among
  Most boring of them all
Keeps taking One More for the Road
  And lives across the hall.

Alice Hamilton

Slight Error

After-Dinner Speaker

Unaccustomed
As he is
To rise
And speak,

He has notes
Enough
To last through
All next week.

Joan Y. Brewton

"C'mon, boy!"

"He ate my net!"

The Silence Was Deafening

1. Mind if I switch off this drama and get the ball game?
2. How about swapping home-packed lunches, sight unseen?
3. Surely you remember, Bert, that I paid you back that fiver last Wednesday?
4. Well, here I am, folks! Now the party can really get started!
5. Sure your suit is wet, but you'll have to admit it was a pretty good April Fool joke, eh, Frank?

Dick Emmons

Instructions I Never Seem to Notice Until—

Before pressing the starter button, check to see that Bar B is fastened securely to Arm C with Cotter Key D. Do not—we repeat, DO NOT—

Caution: Do not use in the vicinity of—

Removal of the protective coating is relatively simple. Merely cut—

At that point, a sure way to keep the entire assembly from falling to pieces in your hands is—

Before beginning, check to see that you have all the parts pictured and described in Folder 13—

Raymond Howard

Exclamations I Wish I Hadn't Exclaimed

1. Charge it!
2. Well, if it isn't old — er — a —
3. Look! They've got one of those Loop-the-Loop rides!
4. O.K., sonny, peg it to me!
5. Let's flip for the check!
6. Here, let me handle the oars!
7. Another round, bartender!
8. Hot ziggety! A rumba!

Dick Emmons

And Then He Says –
(My favorite movie speeches.)

"Wait a minute, Matt. What about the girl?"

"Of all the conceited, bigoted, opinionated, obstinate, stubb – Jerry, you never kissed me like that before!"

"Somewhere out there beyond those stars and the moon lies the answer to our problem."

"He seems like a bright young lad. A bit headstrong, perhaps. What did you say his name was, Richard the Lion-Hearted?"

Paul C. Law

"So this is what I migrated 11,000 miles for."

Daddy Gets Even

"Daddy, I want an ice-cream cone."
"*What's an ice-cream cone, Bobby?*"
"A cone – with ice cream in it. I want one."
"*Why do you want one?*"
"I like them."
"*Why do you like them, Bobby? Why?*"
"Because they're good. I want one."
"*Why, Bobby?*"
"I said, because I'm hungry."
"*Bobby, what's that man doing over there?*"
"He's driving a car, daddy."
"*Why is he driving it?*"
"I don't know why he's driving it, daddy."
"*Why not?*"
"Well, I suppose he wants to go somewhere in it."
"*Where do you think he wants to go, Bobby?*"
"I don't know. How should I know?"
"*Does the man know?*"
"Why, of course."
"*Why, Bobby?*"
"Well, he must know....Daddy, please buy me an ice-
cream cone."
"*What's an ice-cream cone?*"
"I told you. It's a cone with ice cream in it."
"*Why does it have ice cream in it, Bobby?*"
"Because ice cream is good. People like to eat it."
"*All right, Bobby, but there's just one more question
I want to ask.*"
"O.K. Go ahead, daddy."
"*Why?*"

Parke Cummings

Whatever Gave You the Idea I Was Nervous?

Well, our Junior made his first Thespian appearance — school play — the other evening, and of course his proud parents attended. I take pleasure in presenting chronologically the high spots of the drama — curtain goes up at eight P.M. promptly:

8:00 P.M.	Auditorium nearly one quarter full, audience still filing in.
8:43	Curtain goes up.
8:43-9:02	Discourse between various characters.
9:03	Enter Junior.
9:04	Junior delivers first line perfectly: "There's a storm gathering in the east."
9:05	Junior gazes out at audience.
9:06	Junior recognizes parents.
9:08	Heroine asks: "Do you think the flood will reach us?"
9:09	Heroine repeats: "Do you think the flood will reach us?"
9:09½	Heroine repeats, in a loud voice: "Do you think the flood will reach us?" at same time edging toward Junior and eventually nudging him.
9:10	Junior starts violently, and then replies: "We've got to be prepared for anything."
9:11	Exit Junior.
10:15	Act II.
10:27	Enter Junior.
10:28	Junior starts speech: "There comes a time in all our lives when we must — when we must — when we — "
10:29	Silence.
10:29½	Silence punctuated by nervous coughs in the audience.

Here's the Pitch

The long slow curve:

"Honey, don't you think you ought to get yourself one of those new Belgian spinning reels you were talking about, before your next fishing trip? I know they're expensive, but they must be terrific."

"That nosy old Mrs. Johnson was asking me today why you keep buying lathes and things for your workshop when you don't really build much of anything down there, and I certainly told *her* off!"

And the fast break:

"I went to an antique auction today, and — "

Peg Bracken

Spring Is Here

It's not the first robin,
  The last of the snow,
It's the living room stripped,
  The windows aglow;
New paint in the kitchen,
  New wax on the stair,
The rugs in the back yard,
  The dust in the air.
It's not April showers
  That whisper and sing,
It's the riot of cleaning
  That tells me it's spring!

Catherine E. Berry

Motto for a One-Room Apartment

These in-a-wall beds
  Are, in a word, awful,
And ought to be burned
  At the stake as unlawful.

Margaret Fishback

That'll Be the Day

Dear Sir: My son is four months old and I have not yet been approached by a representative of your studio for photographs. I would appreciate it if you would have a salesman call at my home at his earliest convenience.

Mrs. Thomas Coe

Dear Mrs. Lane: I have just been informed that my dog got into your garden and did some damage. The dog will be kept chained to the house and I shall send you a check to compensate for your loss. Please accept my apologies.

Mrs. Ruth Johnson

Marceline Murphy

Training Period

Engine, engine, on the track,
Shunting forward, shunting back,
Must you always halt your freight
At the crossing where I wait?

Betty Isler

My Day Off

The sun shines bright on Monday,
A lovely day for hiking.
The wind blows soft on Tuesday,
A perfect day for biking.

Wednesday, winds are blowing hard;
Good to work out in the yard.
Thursday, there's a frosty nip;
Splendid for a motor trip.

Friday's fine; the warming air
Is grand for golf or bowling.
And Saturday, both warm and fair,
Is excellent for trolling.

Then Sunday dawns:
A tempest breaks;
The wind and rain cut capers.
And all I do
On My Day Off
Is — read the Sunday papers.

E. A. Barnett

Best Solution

I'm learning how to walk again.
It's easier by far
Than coping with two teenage sons,
One daughter — and one car.

Jean Conder Soule

Decisions I Reached Rather Easily

1. "There's going to be some pain involved as I work on this tooth. Do you want to take a good grip on the chair or would you prefer Novocain?"
2. "Honey, the hobby store called to say that Junior's new ten-speed bike has arrived from the factory. Do you want them to assemble it or would you rather do it yourself?"
3. "A committee from the church will be pleased to call on you next Sunday afternoon and explain fully the need for a new educational wing, plus our on-going worldwide mission of concern...or you can just sign your pledge card and mail it in."

Dick Emmons

"This is the only way I can tell which house is mine!"

Parental Viewpoint

The "generation gap" of which
I am most truly chary
Involves...well, like...I mean...you know...
Well, like...vocabulary!

Fred S. Buschmeyer, Jr.

Quick Thinking

"I'm glad they fit you, honey. They're the first slacks I've ever bought you, and I didn't realize at first how large...a selection they had in that store."

"Sure I remember what today is—Monday. But is that any reason to...think I'd forgotten our anniversary?"

"I know this must be something you put in a tie box just to fool me, because if there's one thing I don't need it's...anything expensive."

"The girl back there by the bus stop? Sure, I've known her for years. In fact, she was the first girl I ever ki—...—idded in grammar school. She had millions of freckles, and—"

Hal Tennant

Promises, Promises

If you keep acting this way, my mother will never visit us again!

I'm not going to say one more word on the subject!

Just one moment, please...

I'll certainly never ask you to do anything again!

Dennis W. Nicks

D—eatitude

At the University of Oklahoma, as at many other schools, it is customary for students to leave a self-addressed, stamped postcard with the professor, requesting that he mark on it the final grade for the course. While assisting the professor in recording the grades of one of his classes, we came across a postcard that stated, "Blessed are the merciful." The card was promptly returned with the following inscription, "Blessed are they that mourn, for they shall be comforted. Final Grade: D."

Eleanora Newman

Post Toast

As you slide down the bannister of life, may all the splinters be pointed in the right direction.

Kemmons Wilson

From the Seller's Point of View

"Your house is just LOVEly," they tactfully say
As they traipse through my property day after day,
"The kitchen's diVINE; the porch is nice too!
I guess you are sad to leave, aren't you?"

The weeks slowly pass — I keep waxing the floor,
Hearing their "oooooos" and their "aaaahhs" galore.
If only I DARED, I'd FACE them and CRY it:
"If you LOVE it so much, why the HECK don't you
BUY it?"

Lee S. Rush

Daffy Definitions

VACATION: A period of 2 weeks which are 2 short, afte[r] which you are 2 tired 2 return 2 work and 2 broke not 2.

ORIGINALITY: The art of remembering what you hear and forgetting where you heard it.

DEFICIT: What you have when you haven't as much as when you had nothing.

Lucille Goodyear

Old-Timer's Sunday

The deep-dish pie was deeper that day,
The roasted chicken was plumper;
The afternoon was spent face to face
Instead of bumper to bumper.

Alma Denny

"This should be good."

Have You Thanked a Green Plant Today?

(Bumper Sticker)

Thank you, thank you, lovely plant,
Eye-delighting oxidant.
You gratify the eye, and then,
To top it off, make oxygen.
You beautify, and then, to boot,
(Oh lungs, rejoice) you depollute.
Thank you for this twofold bliss
Wrought by photosynthesis.
(Now I hereby bequeath to you
A life supply of CO_2.)

Don Anderson

Stop, You're Breaking My Heart

MARCH 19, 1946.

MISS JO-AN COLE,
VASSAR COLLEGE.

SPRING FORMAL SET FOR MAY 18 STOP WILL MEET YOU AT STATION STOP TAKE 2:52 TRAIN LOVE BOB

MARCH 30, 1946.

MR. ROBERT SMIRNOW,
DARTMOUTH COLLEGE.

SORRY I CAN'T MAKE IT STOP GLEE CLUB CONCERT THAT NIGHT
LOVE JO-AN

APRIL 14, 1946.

MISS PENNY BROWN,
SMITH COLLEGE.

HONEY OUR BIG SPRING FORMAL FALLS ON MAY 18 THIS YEAR STOP BIG WEEK END TO GO WITH IT STOP LET ME KNOW WHAT TRAIN YOU'RE ARRIVING ON
LOVE BOB

APRIL 26, 1946.

MR. BOB SMIRNOW,
DARTMOUTH COLLEGE.

AM NOT ARRIVING ON ANY TRAIN STOP LAST YEAR WAS TOO INFORMAL TO SUIT ME PENNY

MAY 4, 1946.

MISS MARY CARMICHAEL,
COLBY JUNIOR COLLEGE.

DARLING AM ASKING YOU FIRST DO YOU WANT TO COME TO THE SPRING FORMAL FOR A GALA WEEK END STOP BIG NAME BAND AND LOTS OF FUN STOP LET ME KNOW RIGHT AWAY STOP THAT'S THE WEEK END OF THE 18TH STOP BE WAITING WITH BATED BREATH
BOB SMIRNOW

MAY 10, 1946.

MR. ROBERT SMIRNOW,
DARTMOUTH COLLEGE.

LOVE TO BOB BUT RALPH ASKED ME
FIRST STOP SEE YOU UP THERE
THE COLBY KID

MAY 13, 1946.

MISS ALICIA HAND,
MARY BALDWIN HIGH SCHOOL FOR GIRLS.

BABY DOLL SORRY I'VE WAITED SO LONG
TO ASK YOU KEPT PUTTING IT OFF BUT
THE DARTMOUTH SPRING FORMAL IS ON
THE 18TH STOP PLEASE PLEASE EXCUSE
THE DELAY AND BE MY ONE AND ONLY
FOR THE WEEK END STOP ANSWER
IMMEDIATELY LOVE BOB

MAY 15, 1946.

MR. BOB SMIRNOW,
DARTMOUTH COLLEGE.

OH YOU GREAT BIG HE-MAN YOU STOP WAS
THRILLED BY THE INVITE BUT MISS SPECT
THE HEADMISTRESS SAYS NO STOP I'LL BE
WEEPING IN MY SLEEPING
OCEANS OF EMOTIONS
ALICIA

MAY 15, 1946.

MISS STEPHANIE SMIRNOW,
184 BURNS ST.,
FOREST HILLS, L.I.

SIS HOW WOULD YOU LIKE TO COME TO A GREAT BIG SPRING FORMAL UP HERE AT DARTMOUTH STOP LOTS OF FUN AND LOTS OF FELLOWS STOP LET ME KNOW IF YOU CAN MAKE IT STOP CAN YOU ARRIVE DAY AFTER TOMORROW AND STAY TILL SUNDAY BOB

MAY 16, 1946.

MR. ROBERT SMIRNOW,
DARTMOUTH COLLEGE.

BOB DEAR STEPHANIE'S SWEETIE JUST GOT BACK FROM JAPAN STOP AM ARRIVING ON THE 12 O'CLOCK TRAIN BE THERE TO MEET ME

LOVE MOTHER

Ed Graham, Jr.

“F”

Silence Is Golden

1. “Imagine meeting *you* here!”	1. (“Everybody goes to the bathroom *sometime!*”)
2. “Don’t look now, Dear, but that woman coming toward us should have either a new dye job or a new wig!”	2. (“You’ve never met my mother, have you?”)
3. “What an absolutely scrumptious pie! I just can’t *stand* those frozen things, can you?”	3. (“You’re eating one.”)
4. “No! No! NO! It’s *my* turn to pay the tab!”	4. (“Right you are!”)

Addison H. Hallock

Life's Shortest Moment

I find it hard to comprehend,
In this modern age,
That there exists a speck of time
Too abrupt to gauge.
A fleeting moment so elusive
It's not yet defined;
It exists between the green light
And the horn behind.

R. Kuchenbecker

Guess What's on Your Nose, Dear

The dumbest insect in the world they say's the common fly. His brain is truly tiny and his I.Q. isn't high.

But stupid though the fly may be
He never fails to outwit me,
For, every time I hear one buzz,
I swat not where he's *at*, but *was*!

Addison H. Hallock

Bathtub Banter

The bathtub was invented in 1850 and the telephone in 1875. This probably doesn't mean anything very special, but if you had been living back then, you could have sat in the bathtub for up to 25 years without hearing the telephone ring.

Coffeyville, Kansas, Journal

The Bride Wore—

According to the newspapers: A white-ivory satin duchess gown trimmed with heirloom point lace and a veil of tulle with orange blossoms.

According to the bride's mother: A dress that was bought at the very last minute because, in spite of determined efforts at alteration, the dress which I'd worn in 1908 couldn't be made to fit. It was too bad because it was in perfect condition and looked simply lovely, and don't you think girls are much larger now than they used to be?

According to the bride's father: An outfit that cost seventy-five dollars.

According to the bridesmaids: An outfit that was just a trifle extreme for Marge, but that's Marge for you.

According to the groom: A lot of white stuff.

Louis Jamme

Question for January

Now, why have all the windows got
Such a pretty store of
Things I want an awful lot,
All for sale upon the spot
For such a little bit of what
I haven't any more of?

Wallace Irwin, Jr.

"Admit it — you married me for my money!"

Plea to a Shower Bath

Before I turn your handle to the zone marked "Hot,"
I'll state the things I hope you'll do and some I hope
you'll not.

Pray throw a firm and steady stream; be neither
bold nor fickle.
Resemble not Niagara Falls and yet eschew the
trickle.

And kindly keep your temperature not torrid not
benumbing.
It's no excuse that someone else has tuned in on the
plumbing.

Robert Mattison

Set in Century Expanded, a typeface designed by
Morris Fuller Benton and introduced by American
Typefounders circa 1900. The titles are set in
ITC Souvenir Bold italic, designed by Ed Benguiat.
The paper is Hallmark Eggshell.
Book design: Rick Cusick.